THIS BOOK BELONGS TO

_____

the eclectic witch's BOOK of SHADOWS COMPANION

© BOBBIE HODGES

Deborah Blake is the author of over a dozen books on modern witchcraft, including *The Little Book of Cat Magic* and *Everyday Witchcraft*, as well as the acclaimed *Everyday Witch Tarot* and *Everyday Witch Oracle* decks. Deborah lives in a 140-year-old farmhouse in upstate New York with numerous cats who supervise all her activities, both magical and mundane. She can be found at

DEBORAHBLAKEAUTHOR.COM

the
€CL€CTIC WITCH'S
BOOK *of* SHADOWS
COMPANION
A Workbook
FOR YOUR
Witchy Wisdom

DEBORAH BLAKE

Llewellyn Publications
Woodbury, Minnesota

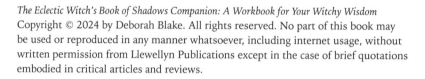

FIRST EDITION
First Printing, 2024

Book design by Rebecca Zins
Cover design by Shira Atakpu
Illustrations by Mickie Mueller

Llewellyn is a registered trademark of Llewellyn Worldwide Ltd.

ISBN 978-0-7387-7480-0

Llewellyn Publications
A Division of Llewellyn Worldwide Ltd.
2143 Wooddale Drive
Woodbury, MN 55125-2989

www.llewellyn.com

Printed in the United States of America

Contents

Invocations and Quarter Calls   111

Spells   123

Magical Recipes   153

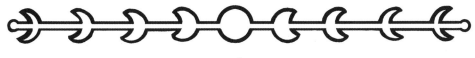

Correspondences   165

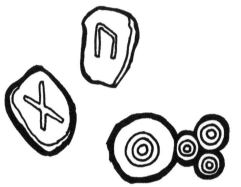

Introduction

If you got *The Eclectic Witch's Book of Shadows* and wished you could take your journey one step further, this workbook is for you. Filled with fun and easy activities, prompts, and suggestions, it also includes additional spells, correspondences, and other information, as well as the opportunity to include your own as you expand your practice. Mickie Mueller provides more fabulous illustrations, as well as coloring pages and plenty of other spaces you can fill in to create your own decorative touches.

The Eclectic Witch's Book of Shadows Companion follows much of the same organization as *The Eclectic Witch's Book of Shadows* for ease of use. Additionally, there are sections with charts to fill in, a goal-oriented Wheel of the Year, crystal grids, instructions for creating your own personal sigil, and numerous places to write down the results of your experiences with everything from spells to tarot readings to recipes. Magical and practical, it is the perfect way to continue working with your own Book of Shadows.

We listened when many of you said you didn't want to write in your beautiful hardcover *Book of Shadows*, and now we've provided you with an alternative that is designed to be practical, usable, and very much your own.

Color!

Write!

Explore!

Enjoy!

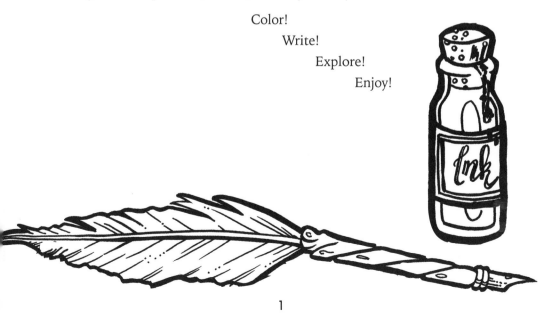

1

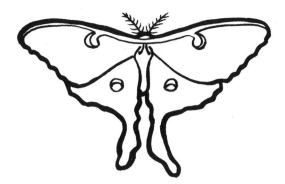

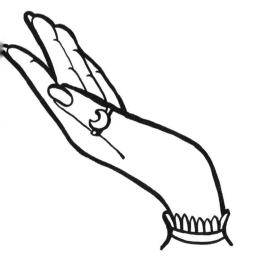

who says
wicked
can't be
good?
~Blake

Herbs

Herbal magic is one of the easiest, safest, and most joyous methods of reestablishing earth roots, of returning to a healthy and natural life. It touches the essence of life itself with simple rituals and few props.

◇◇

Scott Cunningham, *Magical Herbalism:*
The Secret Craft of the Wise

Pick Three

Pick three herbs for protection, prosperity, or love, then try a spell or some kitchen witchery. Write down what you did and the date, and then make a note of anything that happens afterward. Do you feel as though your magic worked? If not, what could you change next time?

Protection: Basil, chamomile, cinnamon, dill, elderberry, eucalyptus, fennel, fern, garlic, geranium (also called rose geranium), juniper, mistletoe, mullein, parsley, rose, rosemary, rowan (tree), rue, St. John's wort, sage, tarragon, vervain

---

Sample Protection Herb Spell
(what your own version might look like)

SPELL: Protect this home and all that live here with these herbs of power strong; keep this place protected all day and all night long.
HERBS USED: rosemary, dill, and garlic hung up in a charm bag by the front door
WHAT HAPPENED? So far so good!
REMINDER: Refresh the spell once a year—maybe add new herbs.

Prosperity: Allspice, angelica, basil, chamomile, cinnamon, clove, dill, ginger, honeysuckle, Irish moss, jasmine, nutmeg, oak (tree), orange, patchouli, peppermint, pomegranate, rosemary, sandalwood, thyme

Love: Apple, basil, bergamot, calendula, carnation, catnip, chamomile, cinnamon, clove, geranium, lavender, lemon, lemon balm, rose, thyme, vanilla, verbena, yarrow

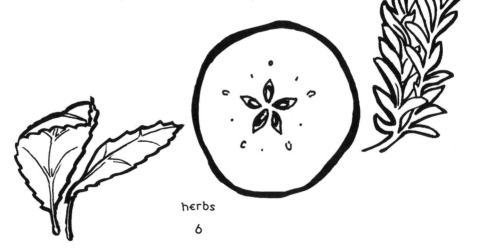

herbs

✧ What did you do? ....

✧ What herbs did you use? ....

✧ What happened afterward? ....

Notes:

✧ What did you do? ....

✧ What herbs did you use? ....

✧ What happened afterward? ....

Notes:

✧ What did you do? ....

✧ What herbs did you use? ....

✧ What happened afterward? ....

Notes:

....

....

....

....

....

....

Do you have a few favorite herbs you find yourself going back to time and again? I do! I love so many, but among my favorites are rosemary, sage, lavender, and peppermint. What are yours?

herbs

What's in Your Cupboard?

Take a look at your kitchen cupboards and spice racks. What do you already own, and what magical work is it good for? Are there any important herbs that are missing? If so, make up a shopping list.

HERB/SPICE	MAGICAL USES

	NEED TO GET

Don't forget to check your yard, if you have one! You might have shrubs, trees, or things growing in a flower or vegetable garden that you can use in your magical work.

herbs

To a large degree, the power of herbs stems from
their strong, uncivilized, independent nature.
When we harness that sort of wild, unregimented
energy for magic, two important things happen.
First, this raw energy acts as a catalyst for our
spells and gives them the impetus necessary to
soar directly into the cosmos and hit their mark.
Second, and as powerful, is that as spellcasters
we automatically receive any residual herbal
energies. They boost our personal power,
increase our magical abilities, and—because of
their connection to the Earth—ground us so
we are able to carry out any mundane actions
necessary to complete the magic at hand.

✧

Dorothy Morrison, *Bud, Blossom & Leaf*

Teas for a Purpose

Teas are an easy way to use magic with nothing more complicated than hot water and either a tea ball or a strainer. (Well, you'd also need a mug or cup, obviously, or it would get very messy.) There are many herbs that are safe to drink that have magical properties, although some of them taste better than others. Herbs can be combined or drunk on their own, and many of them have helpful medicinal benefits as well.

Ten Herbs to Use for Tea

Chamomile (flowers): Healing, peace, sleep, love, protection, prosperity, purification

Cinnamon (stick): Healing, love, lust, power, success, protection, psychic powers, prosperity

Elderberry (berries or juice): Healing, protection, prosperity

Ginger (root): Love, prosperity, success, energy, passion

Lemon (juice or peel): Love, lust, purification, cleansing

Lemon Balm (leaves): Healing, love, success, peace

Peppermint (leaves): Healing, prosperity, love, purification, clarity, sleep

Rose (hips, petals, or rosewater): Love, healing, protection, peace

Tea (leaves): Courage, strength, energy, healing. (Yes, tea is an herb too!)

Valerian (leaves): Healing, sleep, calm, love, purification, protection. Note: This herb is often used medicinally to aid in sleep and calming. Use caution until you know how it affects you. It also smells rather like stinky socks, so you might want to add honey or mix it with other herbs.

You can see that many of these teas have healing properties. That's because herbs have been used for healing since the beginning of time by witches and non-witches alike!

who says wicked can't be good? ~Blake

herbs

Write down which herbs you made teas from
and what you thought of them.

....
....
....
....
....
....
....
....
....
....
....
....
....
....
....
....
....
....

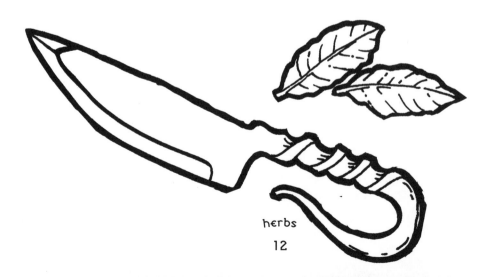

herbs

12

Herbs and garden plants play a meaningful part
in the folklore and tradition of every culture.
Their arcane and phenomenal powers to heal
the mind and body fascinate us and confirm
humankind's connection to the natural world.

❖

Ellen Dugan, *Garden Witchery:*
Magick from the Ground Up

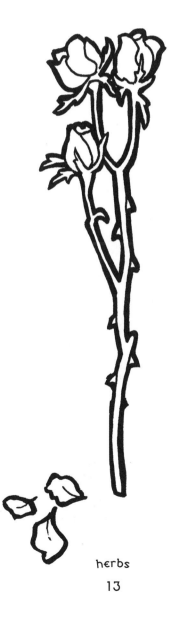

herbs

A Witch's Magical Garden

What makes a garden into a witch's magical garden instead of just a place where you grow tomatoes, flowers, or whatever? Intent, of course.

As with most other aspects of witchcraft, your magical garden is all about what you put into it. I don't mean which plants, although there is that too (back away from the belladonna, please). It comes down to energy and intention, so when you plant your seeds or dig a hole in the dirt for that new fern, you focus on how you plan to use it, and send it love and respect and perhaps a little nudge in the direction of healing or protection or whatever you hope to get back out of it.

Tend your witch's garden well, and once your plants are grown, focus again on intent when you harvest them and prepare the fruits of your labor. And don't worry if you mix your magical plants with the mundane ones—there is very little more magical than a ripe tomato, fresh from the garden. Connecting with nature in multiple ways is part of the reward.

herbs

What's in your garden?

herbs

If you're trying to figure out what herbs to plant and only have space for a few (whether outside in a garden or inside on a sunny windowsill), this handy chart will help you figure out which ones you might find most useful.

Easy Reference Herb Chart

Herbs	Healing/ Purification	Protection	Prosperity	Love
Basil		X	X	X
Chamomile	X	X	X	X
Dill		X	X	X
Lavender	X	X		X
Lemon Balm	X		X	X
Parsley		X	X	X
Peppermint	X		X	X
Rosemary	X	X		X
Sage	X	X		

herbs

Now create your own table for the herbs or plants in your garden/house.

HERBS				

herbs

If you can't have a garden, see if there is a local community garden you can take a plot in, or at least a shop nearby where you can find fresh herbs and plants.

herbs

Your Book of Shadows Notes

....
....
....
....
....
....
....
....
....
....
....
....
....
....
....
....
....
....
....
....
....
....
....
....
....
....

Stones

Stones are gifts of the earth. They are manifestations
of the universal forces of deity, Goddess, God,
and fate, which created all that is, all that was,
and all that has the potential of being.

❖

Scott Cunningham, *Cunningham's Encyclopedia*
of Crystal, Gem & Metal Magic

Less Common Stones and Their Magical Correspondences

In *The Eclectic Witch's Book of Shadows*, I talked about a number of my favorite stones, all of which are common and relatively easy to find. These included agate, amber, amethyst, aventurine, carnelian, citrine, crystal quartz, fluorite, garnet, hematite, jade, jasper, jet, lapis lazuli, malachite, moonstone, onyx, rose quartz, smoky quartz, sodalite, tiger's eye, and turquoise.

This wide variety of gemstones ranges from inexpensive to pricey, but you will probably be able to find most of them at any local Pagan or New Age store, if you are lucky enough to have one, or even at other less specialized shops like health food stores.

You might have to look a little harder for some of my other beloved stones, but I like these ones enough to make the search worth it. A few of my less common favorites include:

Amazonite: A bluish-green stone. Good luck, success, love, calming. Sometimes known as the gambler's stone.

Bloodstone: Green with red spots or flecks. Healing, courage, prosperity, success, power. As its name would imply, it is associated with healing anything to do with the blood, and it's good for when you need to go into any kind of battle (although hopefully not an actual one).

Celestite: Light blue. Healing, calm, anti-stress. Celestite is said to work with the top three chakras (throat, third eye, and crown) and therefore has a beneficial effect on speech, thought, and compassion. Absolutely stunning in crystal form, I use this in healing work a great deal.

Lepidolite: Light purple, often with specks of mica. Healing (especially for the emotions, like stress and depression), calming, helps with change and transitions. When I went through a time of major change recently, I found myself extremely drawn to this stone even though at the time I didn't know what it did.

Obsidian: Black, actually a form of volcanic glass. Grounding, protection, peace, divination. If this stone can survive a volcano, it can probably help you get through the upheavals in your own life.

Rhodocrosite: Pink. Peace, love, positive energy. This pretty, deep pink stone looks great in jewelry.

Selenite: Clear stone with layers, so it looks slightly cloudy. Clarity, energy, purification, peace, calm, positive energy. This stone is useful for clearing and cleansing other stones or tools used in magical work. It is named after Selene, a goddess of the moon, so it is also very good for full moon magic.

Remember to listen to your instincts. If you are drawn to a particular stone (like I was to the lepidolite), it may turn out to be just the thing you need. Do a little research, if you want, to see what the stone is good for, magically speaking—or just get it!

stones

24

Crystal Grids for Different Magical Purposes

A crystal grid is when a number of gemstones are set out in a specific pattern based on what is called sacred geometry. The specific layout can vary from the simple, such as one crystal set in the middle of a number of smaller stones, to arrangements way too complicated and esoteric to get into here. The purpose of a crystal grid is to amplify and strengthen a magical working by placing specific stones into patterns that have universal power.

Some people create their own grids, while others use templates made by someone else (these can be found online). They aren't something I have gotten into in any depth, but I have witchy friends who swear by them. They also have the benefit of being beautiful as well as useful.

If you decide to try experimenting with crystal grids, be sure to set them up on an altar or some other space where they won't be disturbed. Many people set them up on a tray that can be moved easily.

You also will want to cleanse your stones and the space where you'll be using them before getting started to make sure the energy is as pure as possible from the beginning.

Simple designs include three stones in a circle (or triangle) around a central crystal or a box of four with one in the middle. Spiral or labyrinth shapes are also common. It is usual to have the largest stone in the center and get progressively smaller as you move outward, but the only really important thing is that the arrangement resonates with you and feels right. You can use a mix of stones or all one type.

To activate a crystal grid, fix your intention as strongly as possible in your mind, then use your pointing finger to touch each stone, drawing an invisible line of energy that connects them to each other. You can redo this step every few days for as long as you have your grid set up. You will also want to sit with your grid for a few minutes every day.

I've included a few examples you can use as I've laid them out, but you can always substitute different stones for ones you don't have or that don't feel right for you.

stones

25

Crystal Grid 1: General Empowerment of Magic/Self

These stones will also work for courage and energy magic.

Central stone: Crystal quartz

Three surrounding stones: All crystal quartz or one each amethyst, carnelian, and tiger's eye

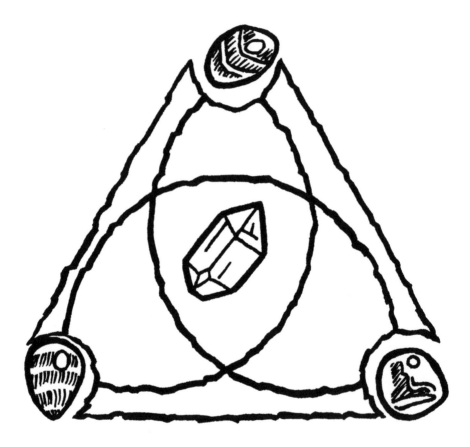

Crystal Grid 2: Love

These stones will also work for friendship, emotional healing, or peace.

Central stone: Amethyst

Four surrounding stones: Crystal quartz, rose quartz, moonstone, lapis

Crystal Grid 3: Prosperity

These stones will also work for abundance, growth, and general earth magic.

Central stone: Crystal quartz

Five surrounding stones: Aventurine, green agate, green jasper, malachite, tiger's eye

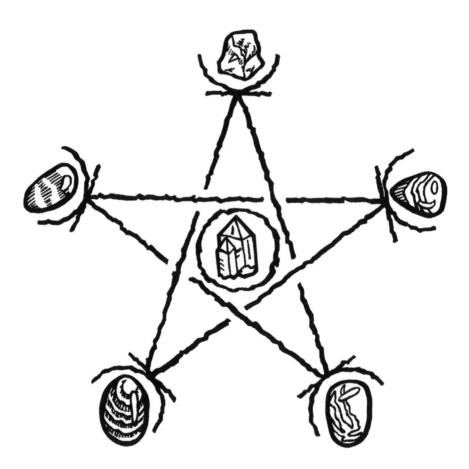

Draw Your Own Crystal Grid

Purpose:

Stones:

stones

Draw Your Own Crystal Grid

Purpose:

Stones:

stones

Draw Your Own Crystal Grid

Purpose:

Stones:

stones

You can read a dozen books about witchcraft and gemstones and none of them will agree completely about the magical associations of any particular rock. They're a great place to start, but in the end you need to trust your gut. Pick up the stones and feel their energy or hold your hand an inch or so above a table of

stones and move it over them to see if one in particular tugs at you. I've had more than one instance when I picked up a rock and realized I didn't want to let it go—that was the one for me. Listen to your inner wisdom.

Stone Jewelry Suggestions

One of the easiest ways to integrate the power of gemstones into your everyday life is to make them into wearable magic—in short, jewelry. For instance, I wear a black onyx ring on the ring finger of my left hand. Many witches believe that black onyx, especially worn on the left hand, is protective for those who are psychic and likely to pick up on the energy around them.

I'm a jewelry maker, as well as a witch and a writer, so I've been making magical jewelry for myself and others for years. I have specific necklaces designed for prosperity, protection, to celebrate the Goddess, and many other purposes. Everyone in my group, Blue Moon Circle, has matching jet and amber necklaces with sterling silver pentacles I made for us, which we wear to rituals. As with any other magical tool you make, you should focus on your intention as you create it.

But you don't have to make your own jewelry to integrate stones into wearable magic. You can buy necklaces made out of your favorite stones, get a crystal drop to hang off a leather thong or silver chain, or wear stones as bracelets, earrings, hair decorations, and more. One of the great things about jewelry is that no one has to know you are wearing it for magical purposes (unless there is a pentacle dangling at the end).

You can either pick out your favorite stones or get something with a specific magical purpose in mind, like prosperity or protection, or see what calls to you the most strongly.

Gemstone Colors and Purposes

The following is just a general guideline, and there are always exceptions, but if you are looking for stones to work toward a specific goal, this is a good place to start.

Green: prosperity, success

Blue: healing, calm

Red/orange: passion, courage, lust, energy

Pink: love, friendship, peace

Black: protection

White/clear: Purification, the Goddess, moon, energy

You can also make regular jewelry into something magical by blessing and consecrating it for whatever purpose you desire, using this simple spell. First, cleanse the stones (see page 36). Once it is cleared of any residual energy, say this spell while holding the jewelry:

Blessed and cleansed

Worn with purpose

Let this _____ (necklace, bracelet, etc.)

Be filled with energy for _____
(purpose such as healing, protection, etc.)

And let it work for my benefit in all positive ways

So mote it be

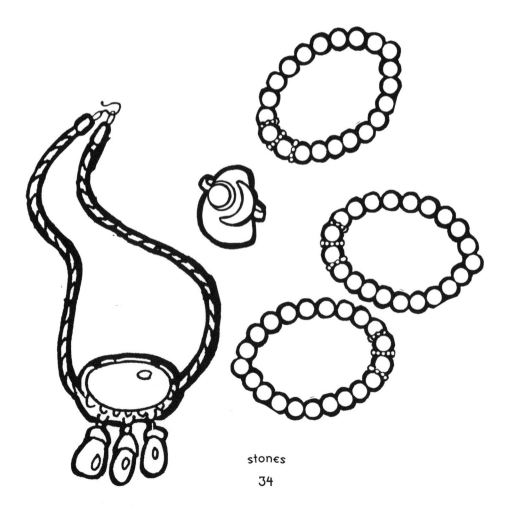

stones

Crystals . . . are
keys possessing the
ability to unlock
psychic and spiritual
powers.

◇

Devin Hunter,
*Crystal Magic
for the Modern Witch*

stones

Cleansing and Clearing Stones

When you are using stones and crystals for magical work, healing, or even just decoration, they can absorb negative energy. Therefore, it is a good idea to periodically cleanse and clear the stones you use. There are a number of simple ways to do this, and you can just choose the ones that work the best for you. Try using different methods of cleansing for your magical stones and see if one seems to be more effective than another. You can track the results here.

Quick Reminder List for Cleansing Options

Before cleansing, check to make sure that your stone doesn't fade in sunlight or wear away in water.

- ✧ moonlight (full moon nights especiallly)
- ✧ sunlight (sacred days like Midsummer especially)
- ✧ water (saltwater or running water)
- ✧ salt
- ✧ sacred smoke
- ✧ you can also try vibrations from ringing a bell or chime, chanting, or whatever else feels right to you

STONE	CLEANSING METHOD	DATE	NOTES

For many centuries and in many cultures,
gemstones have been used to heal and bless.
They have also been employed to manifest a
number of wonderful things, including romance,
abundance, happiness, serenity, and success.

◊◊◊

Tess Whitehurst, *Magical Housekeeping:
Simple Charms and Practical Tips for
Creating a Harmonious Home*

stones

Here is a chart you can use to figure out which stones you might wish to use for various magical intentions.

Easy Reference Stone Chart

Stone	Healing	Love	Prosperity	Protection
Agate, various	X	X	X	X
Amber	X	X	X	X
Amethyst	X	X		X
Carnelian	X	X		X
Clear Quartz	X			X
Jasper, various	X	X	X	X
Lapis	X	X		X
Malachite		X	X	X
Moonstone		X		X
Rose Quartz		X		
Tiger's Eye			X	X

stones

Your Book of Shadows Notes

Candles

There is something special and truly magickal about candlelight. It creates an ambiance that feels different. Cloaked in the gentle glow of the candle, it is easier to put our nine-to-five world aside and think about mystical things.

❖❖

Patricia Telesco, *Exploring Candle Magick:*
Candles, Spells, Charms, Rituals, and Divinations

Candle Magic Spells

Candle magic is one of the simplest, easiest, and fastest types of magic to do. Even the busiest witch can find five minutes to stand at their altar or the kitchen counter and light a candle. At its most basic, a candle magic spell doesn't even need a ritual or any formal wording. All you have to do is light the candle, focus on the light, and speak from the heart.

For example, if you are having a rough day, you can say: *Goddess, please send me the strength to deal with _____.*

Or if you find out someone you care about is ill or injured, you can say: *God and Goddess, please send healing to _____ and watch over them during this difficult time.*

See? Simple. Of course, you can also use candle magic with a more ceremonial spell, if you want. Here's one example:

As the light of this candle goes out into the universe

So goes my wish and my will

As the light of this candle brightens the room

So will magic my wish fulfill

Candle magic can be as simple or as complicated as you want it to be. Try a few different things and write them down here.

....

....

....

....

....

....

candles

Subtle Candle Magic Work

One of the best things about candle magic is that no one has to know you are doing it. If you are someone who isn't out of the broom closet yet or who shares your home with less than sympathetic others, you can still do magical work without anyone being the wiser.

Not only can you do the kind of simple spells I mentioned in the previous section—which can be done in a moment, without saying the words out loud, so it just looks like you are lighting a candle and standing there for an extra minute—you can also add subtle magical touches that either won't be noticed or will be dismissed as merely decorative.

Here are a few examples:

⟡ Very lightly scratch symbols or words into the candle, then smooth them over with your fingers. The warmth of your hands will make them practically disappear.

⟡ Tie a colored ribbon around the base in a color that matches the magical work you're doing. You might also use a small decorative wreath of flowers appropriate to your intent.

⟡ When no one is around, anoint the candle with a few drops of magical oil. The smell will barely be noticeable, and anyone who smells it will simply assume you are using a scented candle.

⟡ Place a crystal in front of the candle to boost its energy. Most people will assume it is just a pretty rock.

I find using candles incredibly uplifting. Just the act of lighting the wick and bringing that glow into a darkened room feels magical. Don't forget to focus on the power of this simple act, and remember that witches have been doing the same thing for thousands of years.

candles

46

Some Candle Cautions

✧ Never leave a burning candle unattended.

✧ Never go to bed and leave a candle burning.

✧ Be cautious using candles around pets. They can burn themselves or knock over the candle and set things on fire.

✧ Make sure your candle is in a fire-safe container away from anything flammable like paper, cloth (curtains, etc.), or oils.

✧ Be careful when using scented candles. Unless they are made with essential oils, they can cause issues in sensitive people. Also, since the scents aren't made from natural sources, they won't add power to your magic in the way that essential oils made from plants would.

For magic to exist, it must be shared. Always remember to pass along your kindness to others . . . A candle loses nothing by lighting another candle.

◇◇◇

Michael Delaware, *Blue and the Magical Forest: The Power of Hopes and Dreams*

candles

Mind Your Beeswax

Most of the candles we use are made from paraffin. They are inexpensive and easy to find, and almost all of the readily available candles in stores (even New Age and Pagan stores) are made out of it. I use them myself. The downside of paraffin is that it is a petroleum product and therefore not exactly natural.

A great alternative, if you can find it, is beeswax. Beeswax candles burn more slowly, last longer, and have a beautiful light honey scent. And, of course, they come from bees, who are associated with the Goddess. Craft stores sometimes have rolls of beeswax you can use to make your own, and of course you can find beeswax candles online if there aren't any available locally. I like to keep some beeswax votives around for spells that call for something special.

For another natural option, there are also candles made from soy wax.

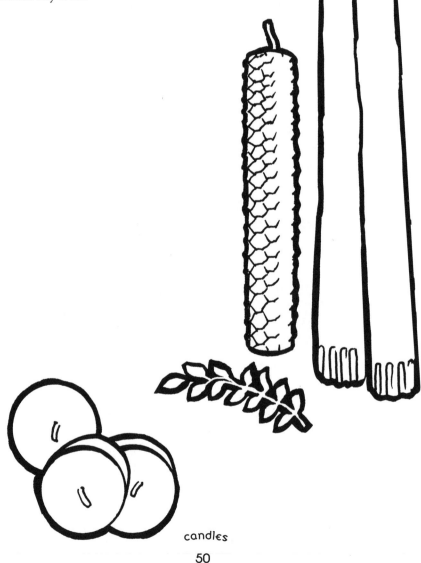

candles

Candle Color Correspondences

Candle color correspondences are much like those for stones or any other color-related witchcraft. You can refer to those charts or check the one specifically for candles on page 71 of the original *Eclectic Witch's Book of Shadows*. To take your practice to the next level, try keeping a spell log to track what you did with your candle magic. Make a note of colors, shape or type of candle, how many you used, how long you let them burn, and any extras such as symbols etched into the candles or oils you anointed them with. You might also want to make a note of whether or not you felt the spell was successful or if there was something you wished you had done differently.

Candle Spell Chart

Color	Shape/Type	# Used	Burn Time

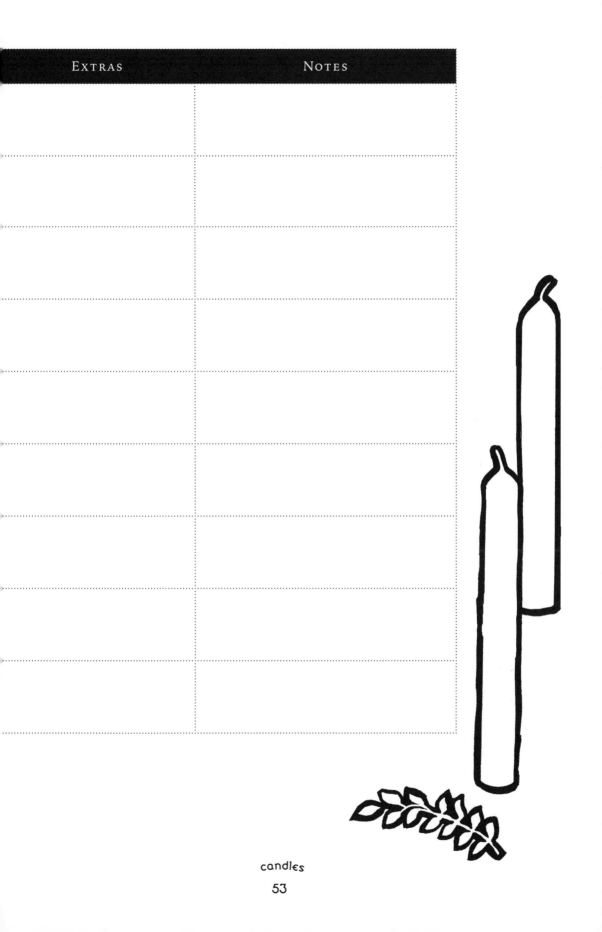

candles

candles

Your Book of Shadows Notes

....
....
....
....
....
....
....
....
....
....
....
....
....
....
....
....
....
....
....
....
....
....
....
....
....

Crafty Recipes

When our own energy is concentrated and channeled, it can move the broader energy currents. The images and objects used in spells are the channels, the vessels through which our power is poured and by which it is shaped. When energy is directed into the images we visualize, it gradually manifests physical form and takes shape in the material world.

❖

Starhawk, *The Spiral Dance: A Rebirth of the Ancient Religion of the Great Goddess*

Creating Your Own Personal Sigil

At its most basic, a sigil is a symbol used in magic. It may be inscribed or drawn on paper or an object to represent a word, intent, or, in this particular case, you. The word comes from the Latin for "seal" (like the type that is used to make an impression in melted wax to seal a letter).

A personal sigil is a design that is used to symbolize your magical self. It can be used as something like a signature (in your Book of Shadows, for instance) or can be etched into a candle or drawn onto a spell page to indicate that the spell is yours, in which case it is a way of directing energy.

There are many ways to make a personal sigil, some of which are quite complicated. The way I was taught uses your name, whether your everyday name or your magical name. Since my magical name is Onyx, it was actually quite simple to make a sigil out of it. If the name you are using is long, some approaches suggest using only the consonants and leaving out the vowels, or leaving out duplicates of any letter that appears more than once. As always, there is no wrong way to do this.

When I made mine, I started with the **O**, which looks like a circle. Then I put the **N** inside the circle so it looked as though the circle was bisected by the lines of the N. Over that, I put the **Y** and then the **X**, which gave me the symbol that stood for my name.

When you make your own, you can doodle around with it until it looks right to you. Some people add a symbol that stands for an animal or use their initials. Just remember that there is power in a sigil, and it will manifest that power for you in your spellwork.

Sigils also can be used to create symbols that represent a goal or intent while doing a spell. For instance, if you wanted to make a sigil that stands for money to etch onto a candle or draw on an herbal charm bag, you could try something like this:

You can sketch out some ideas of your own or practice your name on the following pages.

Crafty Experiments to Try

The original *Eclectic Witch's Book of Shadows* had lots of suggestions for magical recipes, including creating magical oils, charm bags, and poppets. But that's just the tip of the iceberg—or the witch's hat, if you will. There are all sorts of crafty hobbies that lend themselves to the practice of witchcraft.

Here are a few possibilities to try:

⬦ Magical potpourri: It's not unusual to find potpourri in people's houses. But you can add a magical twist by making one with a purpose. For instance, if you wish to bring peace and love to your home, you could fill a pretty jar or bowl with dried rose petals or rose buds (or both), lavender, chamomile flowers, calendula flowers, and sticks of cinnamon. It will look beautiful, smell good, and carry your intention into the very air you breathe.

⬦ Seasonal wreaths: Wreaths aren't just for Christmas. Some crafty folks like to make different ones for every season, and as a witch, you can do the same, but with that extra bit of magical flair. You could make one for each sabbat, for instance, integrating elements from the holiday into your wreath. Most craft stores sell grapevine bases that you can decorate with dried corn, gourds, and leaves for Mabon or holly and mistletoe for Yule. The only limit is your imagination.

⬦ If you like knot magic, try doing macrame and working your magic into that. You can add beads or other decorative elements as well.

⬦ Spell jars are a fun and easy way to invent your own magical recipe. Witch jars were originally intended to protect against witches, but these days we use them to protect against everything else. After I moved into my house, I crafted one and buried it under the bricks outside the entrance door. Making a spell jar is easy. You start with a jar, obviously—one that has a sturdy lid. It can be any size you like, from a tiny miniature to a basic pint canning jar. It doesn't have to be fancy because it will probably be tucked away someplace where no one can see it. Figure out your intention. In the case of my witch jar, I was working toward protection for my house and all those within it. I used some traditional ingredients—dried rosemary, sage, and basil; sea salt; some cloves of garlic; a piece of red jasper; a pin—and put them inside while focusing on my intention. Then I sealed the jar (I think I used melted wax, but it was over twenty years ago, so I don't remember!), blessed and consecrated it, and buried it. As far as I can tell, it is still working!

Think about the kinds of crafty things you like to do and how you might be able to put a magical twist on them. They can be practical or decorative or creative. You can even do them with your kids or your friends for a fun afternoon or evening of magical crafting.

What did you do? Write it down here, with instructions. Tape or glue in pictures if you want.

Sometimes all that's necessary
to turn a rather ordinary
BoS into something great is
a little bit of elbow grease
and a few easily acquired
items at a craft store.

❖

Jason Mankey, *The Witch's Book of
Shadows: The Craft, Lore & Magick
of the Witch's Grimoire*

Magical Goals and Techniques

Magical goals can be approached in any number of ways, and different techniques may work better for some things than for others. One of the things a witch might use their Book of Shadows for is to keep track of what various types of witchcraft they've attempted. You might also want to make notes on whether or not you felt the work was successful or not. This can be as simple as putting an X through the things that didn't give you the results you'd hoped for. You can always write down any thoughts in more detail.

This chart is one way to do that. I've put in a few examples, but you can fill it in any way you like. Obviously, you're not going to use all of these approaches for every spell you do, but you can keep track of which ones you've tried and jot down notes afterward. Maybe write down the date you did the work and at what point you saw results, if any.

Goals and Techniques Chart

GOAL	SPELL	POPPET	KITCHEN WITCHERY
example: healing			chicken soup w/herbs

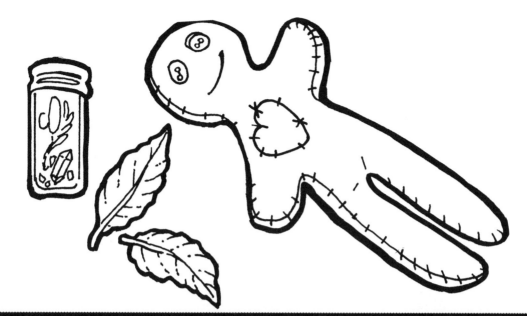

Candle Magic	Charm Bag	Other	Date/Notes
		full moon bath	

Your Book of Shadows Notes

....

....

....

....

....

....

....

....

....

....

....

....

....

....

....

....

....

....

....

....

....

....

....

....

Divination

"Divination" comes from the word "divine." The divine, however you conceive it, usually includes the higher power that can guide you to your best possible life. The act of divination allows you to tap into that divine wisdom and love, to ask questions of it, and to incorporate it into your decision-making process.

◇◇◇

Barbara Moore, *What Tarot Can Do for You: Your Future in the Cards*

Rune Symbols and Meanings

Although many witches use tarot or oracle decks, runes can be just as satisfying—and, depending on who you are, possibly easier to use. Here is a basic chart of the various rune symbols and meanings. Keep in mind that these can vary in spelling from one source to another.

ᚠ	Fehu	wealth, possessions, abundance, fulfillment
ᚢ	Uraz	strength, health/healing, will, tenacity
ᚦ	Thurisaz	luck, new possibilities, awakening, breaking down boundaries
ᚨ	Ansuz	speech, wisdom, advice, inspiration, signals
ᚱ	Raidho	movement, journey, rational growth and change
ᚲ	Kenaz	opening up, hearth or fire, creativity, transformation
ᚷ	Gifu	gifts, partnership, blessings
ᚹ	Wunjo	joy, happiness, harmony, love
ᚺ	Hagall	disruption, delays, limitations, forces outside your control
ᚾ	Nied	patience, passing through a difficult learning experience, delay, learning
ᛁ	Isa	standstill, cease of activities, freeze, wait
ᛃ	Jera	rewards, karma, good harvest, abundance, reaping just rewards
ᛇ	Eihwaz	delay, obstacles, defense, letting go, protection
ᛈ	Perdro	secrets, mysteries, unexpected gains and surprises, psychic powers
ᛉ	Eolh	protection, friendship, fortunate new influence, instincts

ᛋ	SIGEL	power, success, victory, health and vitality
↑	TIR	strength, warrior, male, extreme motivation, increase in power or money
ᛒ	BEORC	birth, new beginnings, new love, growth, renewal, life changes, fertility, family
ᛗ	EHWAZ	travel, physical movement, shifts and changes, steady progress
ᛉ	MANNAZ	cooperation, humankind, knowledge, interdependence, good advice
ᚱ	LAGAZ	imagination, female, intuition and intuitive knowledge
ᛝ	ING	success, relief, milestone events, ending an old phase and beginning another
ᚼ	DAEG	breakthrough, growth, drastic change, awakening, increase and growth
ᛟ	OTHEL	abundance, possessions, inheritance
	WYRD (BLANK)	the unknowable, fate, faith, trust, it is in the hands of the gods

Wyrd or Not?

Wyrd is a blank rune that comes with most sets. It is a fairly new addition to runestones, and some people choose not to use it. Essentially, it is a wild card, meaning anything from "It is in the hands of the gods; wait and see" to "No answer right now."

Rune Readings

Unlike tarot readings, rune readings tend to be fairly basic. The runes lend themselves more to uncomplicated questions with simple answers. You want to make sure that any question you ask is clear and specific: for instance, "Should I take this job?" or "Is now a good time to buy a new house?" A tarot reading might be able to cover both those questions at the same time, but runestones are a little less flexible.

Generally, one does a reading in either of two ways—place all the runestones upside down on the surface you are using, mixing them up as you do so, or place them in a drawstring bag, shake them up, and then stick your hand inside. If they are spread out, try moving your hand over them with your palm facing down until one calls to you. If you are using a bag, just stick your hand in and pull one out. No peeking. No matter which approach you use, it is best to start out with a small number of stones, somewhere between one and three, until you are more comfortable with using them. Even when you are, I find that a runestone reading rarely needs more than four.

Like tarot cards, runes can be read either upright or reversed, so be careful when you lay them out. I find it best to pick all the stones you are using, then go through them one at a time during the reading.

Try these different ways of reading runes. Don't forget to write down both the question you asked and the results you got.

One rune: This is good for yes/no questions or open-ended questions like "What do I need to know today?"

Three runes: For simple yes/no questions, turn over all the runes at once and look at the cumulative answer. If the runes are mostly positive, the answer is probably yes. Sometimes it is more like "Yes, but there will be this kind of difficulty." For more complicated questions, the first rune can be seen as the issue at hand, the second as the suggestion for how to deal with it, and the third as the prediction for what will happen if you do so. Three-rune readings can also be past/present/future.

Which approach you pick depends on you and what you feel will work best for your situation.

Date	Question	Runes Pulled	Interpretation

Date	Question	Runes Pulled	Interpretation

The power of keeping the runes relevant in
a modern context doesn't lie in changing
their meaning to suit our contemporary
purposes but in finding how their layers
of meaning still apply to everyday life.

⸎

S. Kelley Harrell, *Runic Book of Days:*
A Guide to Living the Annual Cycle of Rune Magick

Rune Chart for Tracking
a Month of Rune Pulls

One of the best ways I've found to get comfortable with using runestones is to pull one every morning and write down what it says, then compare it with how your day went. It's a fun and easy way to learn which stones are which, even if you have to look them up each time to begin with. In case you want to try that, here's a chart you can use to keep track of it.

day	rune	result
1		
2		
3		
4		
5		
6		
7		
8		
9		
10		
11		
12		
13		
14		
15		
16		
17		
18		
19		
20		
21		
22		
23		
24		
25		
26		
27		
28		
29		
30		
31		

Oracle Chart for Tracking a Month of Card Pulls

Oracle cards look a lot like tarot cards in that they feature beautiful imagery and often have a theme of some sort that runs through the deck. Most people find them easier to use than tarot, since the cards tend to be more obvious, and often the meanings are spelled out in an accompanying booklet. I find them to be useful for guidance and simple reminders of the things I should have been paying attention to but maybe wasn't.

Like runestones, oracles are rarely used for elaborate readings with multiple cards. They're also something you can use without any kind of learning curve, unlike tarot, which can take a while to master.

In my own deck, the *Everyday Witch Oracle*, I suggest pulling one card for guidance, inspiration, exploration, divination, magical work, or even just for fun. There is absolutely nothing wrong with using the cards for fun. Yes, they can be a serious tool for divination, but who says divination can't be fun too?

If you need more information, you can use two cards for past and present, today and tomorrow, or inspiration. Three cards are useful for past/present/ future, maiden/mother/crone, or you can just pull three random cards and see if they come together to tell you something important.

Or, as with runestones, you can pull one card every day for a month and see if there is any kind of pattern that is revealed over time. For instance, if the same card shows up multiple times, I would say the universe is definitely trying to tell you something!

Here are a few handy charts to use to track a month's worth of card pulls if you decide to try this. While you could always use a number of different decks (which might turn up some interesting patterns in its own way), it might be easier to start out using one deck the first time you do this.

day	card	meaning
1		
2		
3		
4		
5		
6		
7		
8		
9		
10		
11		
12		
13		
14		
15		
16		
17		
18		
19		
20		
21		
22		
23		
24		
25		
26		
27		
28		
29		
30		
31		

Oracle deck used: _____

day	card	meaning
1		
2		
3		
4		
5		
6		
7		
8		
9		
10		
11		
12		
13		
14		
15		
16		
17		
18		
19		
20		
21		
22		
23		
24		
25		
26		
27		
28		
29		
30		
31		

Tarot is always whispering to you. Tarot weaves truth, stories, secrets, and tales. All you need to do is slow down and listen.

◊◊◊

Sasha Graham, *Tarot Diva: Ignite Your Intuition, Glamourize Your Life, Unleash Your Fabulousity!*

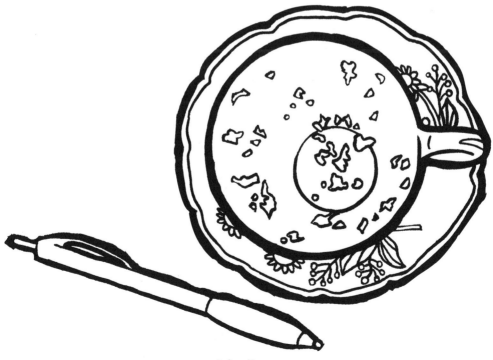

divination

Tarot Reading Charts for One-Card, Three-Card, and Celtic Cross Readings

Tarot cards can be more complicated than runes or oracles, but don't let that intimidate you. They also give you much more scope for using intuition and listening to your inner voice, and if you get confused, most decks come with helpful guidebooks.

Remember to have fun and keep an open mind, and you might be surprised at how well they work for you. If one deck doesn't seem to resonate with you, try a different one. There are literally thousands (including mine), and one of them is sure to fit your style.

If you have a basic question, a one-card pull often works as well as a complicated spread. Simply ask your question and pick a card at random.

For a slightly deeper dive, try a three-card reading. I usually pull one card for past (what led to the situation you are asking about), one for the present (where you are now), and one for the future (where you are going to end up or a suggestion for what you need to do for a positive outcome).

If you want a more detailed reading, the one I usually use is called the Celtic Cross. This uses ten cards (occasionally eleven, if you pull a card out of the deck to stand for the person the reading is for) set up in a specific pattern. Different people lay this pattern out in slightly different ways, but it is always essentially the same thing. I have found it very helpful for people who have more complicated issues that they need answers to.

Reading for Yourself or Others

Many folks who read tarot on a regular basis have discovered over the years that they are either good at reading for others and terrible at reading for themselves (I'm one of those) or the other way around. Some people, of course, are good at both. But don't worry if you only seem to have the gift for one or the other. That's perfectly normal.

One-Card Readings

Deck

Card

....

Date

....

Question

....

Interpretation

....

Deck

Card

....

Date

....

Question

....

Interpretation

....

Deck

Card

....

Date

....

Question

....

Interpretation

....

Three-Card Readings

Deck .... Date ....

Question ....

Cards

Interpretation

....

....

Deck .... Date ....

Question ....

Cards

Interpretation

....

....

Deck   Date
....

Question
....

Cards

Interpretation
....
....

Deck   Date
....

Question
....

Cards

Interpretation
....
....

Celtic Cross Reading 1

Deck   Date

....

Question

....

Card 1 (general environment/atmosphere—base)

....

Card 2 (conflicts & obstacles; may contain potential for growth)

....

Card 3 (foundation/basis for the situation/past/roots)

....

Card 4 (the past/what is passing out of influence)

....

Card 5 (your goals/aims/ideals/outside influences affecting your future)

....

Card 6 (the future; what lies ahead; what you put out into the world)

....

Card 7 (how you see yourself; your conditions & attitudes at the time of the reading)

....

Card 8 (your environment; what surrounds you; how others see you)

....

Card 9 (your hopes & fears of attaining the goal; inner emotions; lessons to be learned)

....

Card 10 (outcome/resolution/result of path taken)

....

Additional cards (questions & clarification)

....

....

divination

Celtic Cross Reading 2

Deck   Date

....

Question

....

Card 1 (general environment/atmosphere—base)

....

Card 2 (conflicts & obstacles; may contain potential for growth)

....

Card 3 (foundation/basis for the situation/past/roots)

....

Card 4 (the past/what is passing out of influence)

....

Card 5 (your goals/aims/ideals/outside influences affecting your future)

....

Card 6 (the future; what lies ahead; what you put out into the world)

....

Card 7 (how you see yourself; your conditions & attitudes at the time of the reading)

....

Card 8 (your environment; what surrounds you; how others see you)

....

Card 9 (your hopes & fears of attaining the goal; inner emotions; lessons to be learned)

....

Card 10 (outcome/resolution/result of path taken)

....

Additional cards (questions & clarification)

....

....

Celtic Cross Reading 3

Deck .... Date ....

Question

....

Card 1 (general environment/atmosphere—base)

....

Card 2 (conflicts & obstacles; may contain potential for growth)

....

Card 3 (foundation/basis for the situation/past/roots)

....

Card 4 (the past; what is passing out of influence)

....

Card 5 (your goals/aims/ideals/outside influences affecting your future)

....

Card 6 (the future; what lies ahead; what you put out into the world)

....

Card 7 (how you see yourself; your conditions & attitudes at the time of the reading)

....

Card 8 (your environment; what surrounds you; how others see you)

....

Card 9 (your hopes & fears of attaining the goal; inner emotions; lessons to be learned)

....

Card 10 (outcome/resolution/result of path taken)

....

Additional cards (questions & clarification)

....

....

Dream Journals

Dreams are usually just our subconscious working to process our day, but they may also be messages from the universe, the gods, or our spirit guardians. If you have a dream that seems significant, it can be helpful to write it down before you forget it, and then revisit it later to see if it has turned out to have special meaning. Here are some extra pages to use for that, if you are so inclined. Don't forget that in addition to simply writing down what you can remember of the dream, you can draw any images that seemed important or that you couldn't figure out at the time.

Your Book of Shadows Notes

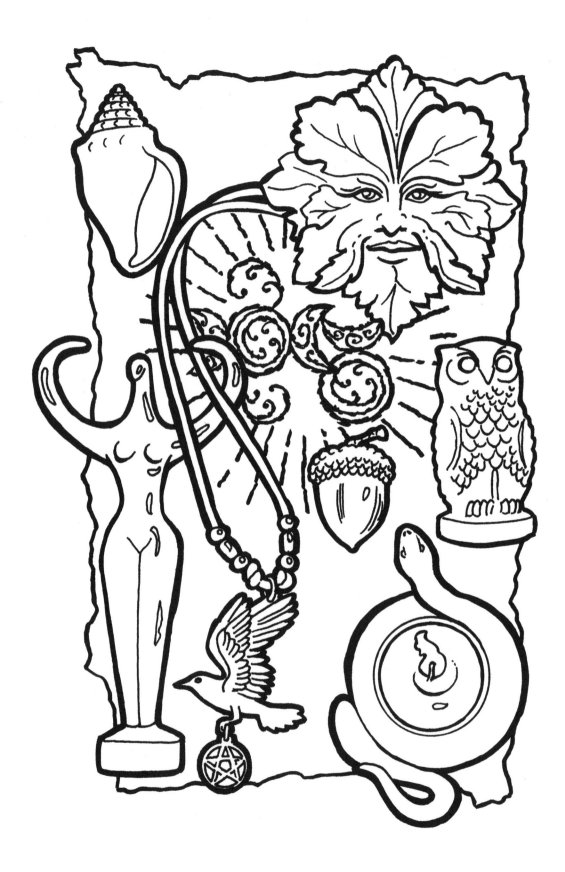

Gods and Goddesses

Everywhere in nature is both male and female, both in the animal kingdom and in the plant kingdom. It seems only natural, therefore, that the deities would be both male and female. The Christian concept of a lone all-male deity does not make sense. Many Wiccan traditions think in terms of a balance between the two energies, while others place more emphasis on one over the other.

❖

Raymond Buckland, *Wicca for Life:
The Way of the Craft from Birth to Summerland*

Figuring Out Who to Worship

For some witches, this isn't even a question. Your deity or deities may come to you clearly from the very start of your journey, tap you on the shoulder, and say hi. For others, like me, it is obvious that there is a Goddess and a God, and you can feel their presence strongly, but not as any particular individual deity. Or you may just sense a power greater than you and leave it at that.

But if you have a desire to find some particular goddess and/or god, or you have the feeling that something out there is trying to send you a message, you can do a few different things to try identifying a deity with whom you have a special connection.

Read and research. Start by reading about various different gods and goddesses. Don't necessarily limit yourself to the ones most of us are most familiar with (Greek, Roman, maybe a few Celtic). Check into deities from your ancestral heritage, whatever that might be. See if any one in particular resonates with you.

Think about the kind of deity you are looking for. Do you want one that is comforting and warm (like Kuan Yin or one of the mother goddesses)? Or do you want someone kick-ass who will help push you to do more (like Artemis or Thor)? If you are in need of healing or protection, look at deities who are known for those qualities.

Open your mind and heart. Stand in front of your altar or under the full moon or just take a walk in the forest or on a beach, and send out the message that you are looking for your personal deity. Then be open to what happens in the days that follow.

....

....

....

....

....

....

....

....

....

....

....

gods and goddesses

Exercises for Connecting with Deity

There are times when the gods will reach out to you, but mostly it will be you reaching out to them. Here are a few suggestions for ways to do that.

⋄ Light a candle and say hello (politely, of course).

⋄ If you have an altar, leave offerings in their honor. Alternately, you can leave offerings somewhere outside. These can be flowers or gifts of food or anything connected to a particular deity.

⋄ Pray. They're listening, I promise. (Although you may not get an obvious response. On the other hand, you might. You never know.)

⋄ If you are trying to connect with a goddess, the night of the full moon is almost always a good time. (Hecate is the one major exception—connect with her during the dark moon.) If you are trying to connect with a sun god, try noon or one of the sabbats. And forests and woods are great places to connect with the wild deities such as Cernunnos, Herne, or Artemis.

⋄ Do good deeds in their names—not with any expectation of reward but as a way of channeling their presence in the world. I try and manifest Goddess energy in the way I take care of nature, do nice things for others, and generally live my life.

If you like, you can use this space to write down what you did and if you felt anything in response.

....

....

....

....

....

....

....

....

....

....

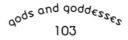

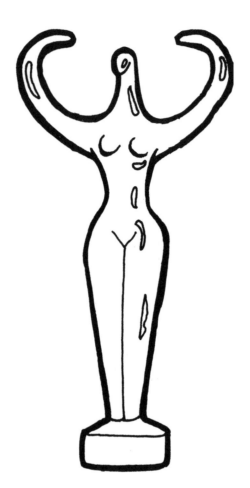

Who is She? She is your power, your Feminine source.
Big Mama. The Goddess. The Great Mystery. The web-
weaver. The life force. The first time, the twentieth time
you may not recognize her. Or pretend not to hear. As
she fills your body with ripples of terror and delight.
But when she calls you will know you've been called.
Then it is up to you to decide if you will answer.

◇◇◇

Lucy H. Pearce, *Burning Woman*

Creating an Altar

Whether you follow a particular deity or just worship Goddess and God in general, it is a nice idea to set up an altar in your home. This is something done in many cultures, including Japanese, Greek, and Roman. These altars might have been for household gods, ancestors, or even sacred spirit guardians.

A deity altar can be as simple or as complicated as you desire. If you only have a tiny space, you may want something very basic, like a picture or statue, a candle or incense holder, and nothing more. Alternately, some people have a more elaborate display, with a special cloth, statues for Goddess and God (mine are very primitive-looking clay figures crafted by my first high priestess, with twig antlers for the God and upraised arms for the Goddess; statues don't necessarily have to be fancy or look like the deity they are meant to represent), candles, incense holders, crystals, shells, feathers, copper offering bowls, and so on.

There is no wrong way to do this as long as you create your altar with reverence and love. If something doesn't feel right to you, just take it off. If something feels like it is missing, try to figure out what it is.

An altar is a great place to leave offerings, light a candle in thanks or to ask for assistance, and it also helps to serve as a reminder that the gods are with you always.

Looking for Signs and Symbols

If you follow a particular deity or are wanting to find one, keep your eyes open for signs and symbols. Most goddesses and gods are associated with specific animals or plants or even insects. If ravens start showing up in your yard every day, that might be a sign—or if a rose starts blooming where you didn't plant one, or there are suddenly lots of bees . . . Part of being a witch is paying attention to the world around you. If someone is sending you a message, you want to make sure you get it!

Your Book of Shadows Notes

Invocations and Quarter Calls

Invoking the Goddess is simply requesting her presence.
The magic is in your head and heart, and in your firm
belief that whatever you truly need is already here.

◊◊◊

Eileen Holland and Cerelia,
A Witch's Book of Answers

Creating Your Own Quarter Calls

Quarter calls are another name for invoking the spirits of the elements. We call them quarter calls because each element is associated with a direction, or quarter: air is east, fire is south, water is west, and earth is north. Each element also has its own associations so that when you create a quarter call, you might integrate some of those into your invocation. Some of this is covered in the original *Eclectic Witch's Book of Shadows* starting on page 157.

Even after all these years, I sometimes find I have to look up the basics of quarter associations or remind myself what I've used in the past as symbols for the elements. So here's a handy chart you can use as a cheat sheet and also as a way of keeping track of what you've done in the past.

Quarter Call Cheat Sheet

Element	Direction	Color	Associations	What You Use
Air	East	Yellow	Communication, knowledge, wind, breath, intellect, thought, new beginnings	
Fire	South	Red	Creativity, passion, energy, flames, the sun, courage	
Water	West	Blue	Emotions, love, intuition, flexibility, cleansing, rain, oceans, rivers, purification	
Earth	North	Green or Brown	Nature, growth, prosperity, grounding, plants, rocks, the body	

Here is some space for you to write down any quarter calls you come up with so you can use them again in the future.

....

....

....

....

....

....

....

....

....

....

....

....

....

....

....

....

....

....

....

....

....

....

....

....

....

....

....

....

....

Fill-in-the-Blank Quarter Calls

If you want to keep things really simple, you can use this basic fill-in-the-blanks form for quarter calls. For example:

> *I summon and invoke the spirit of <u>the east</u>, the power of <u>air</u>. You who are <u>thought</u> and <u>communication</u> and <u>the sweet spring breeze</u>. Come to me now and <u>blow away confusion</u>, <u>leaving only clarity and calm</u>.*

You can see how you can use this basic pattern for any quarter call, changing it for the particular element and its associations. You may use different aspects of each element depending on the occasion and the intent of your spell or ritual.

> *I summon and invoke the spirit of*
> *_____ , the power of _____ .*
>
> *You who are _____ and*
> *_____ and _____ .*
>
> *Come to me now and _____*
> *_____ .*

> *I summon and invoke the spirit of*
> *_____ , the power of _____ .*
>
> *You who are _____ and*
> *_____ and _____ .*
>
> *Come to me now and _____*
> *_____ .*

> *I summon and invoke the spirit of*
> *_____ , the power of _____ .*
>
> *You who are _____ and*
> *_____ and _____ .*
>
> *Come to me now and _____*
> *_____ .*

I summon and invoke the spirit of
_____, *the power of* _____.

You who are _____ *and*
_____ *and* _____.

Come to me now and _____

_____.

When you are doing quarter calls and invocations, it is fine to write things down ahead of time if you are more comfortable with that, or just speak from the heart if that's what works best for you. If you like ornate and flowery language, by all means use it. If you would rather keep things simple, that's fine too. As long as you are respectful and grateful, the words are less important than the magic you are working.

Creating Your Own Invocations

Invoking the gods is a little bit different from calling the quarters. You can summon the elements (politely), but gods should be invited (even more politely and with reverence). They may or may not choose to respond, although honestly, I've never known a time when they haven't.

You can see plenty of invocation examples in the original *Eclectic Witch's Book of Shadows*. Here is a good place to write down any you come up with.

Let my worship be within the heart that rejoices,
for behold, all acts of love and pleasure are
my rituals. Therefore, let there be beauty and
strength, power and compassion, honor and
humility, mirth and reverence within you.

❖

Doreen Valiente, *Charge of the Goddess*

Fill-in-the-Blank Invocations

Like the quarter calls, you can use a basic pattern for invoking the Goddess and God. You can stick to something very simple, like this one:

> *Great Goddess, great God, I greet you and welcome*
> *you to my sacred space. Welcome and blessed be.*

If you are calling on specific gods, you can insert the names of particular deities.

On the other hand, you may wish to use something more elaborate and change the invocation depending on the season, occasion, and the deities you are invoking. If you look at the invocations in *The Eclectic Witch's Book of Shadows*, you can see numerous examples of how this can work. This is a good place to write down your own invocations when you come up with them.

> *I invoke _____, god/dess of*
> *_____. You who are _____*
> *and _____. I call you and ask*
> *that you join me in my sacred space (optional: as*
> *I work on _____ or for*
> *my celebration of _____).*

> *I invoke _____, god/dess of*
> *_____. You who are _____*
> *and _____. I call you and ask*
> *that you join me in my sacred space (optional: as*
> *I work on _____ or for*
> *my celebration of _____).*

> *I invoke _____, god/dess of*
> *_____. You who are _____*
> *and _____. I call you and ask*
> *that you join me in my sacred space (optional: as*
> *I work on _____ or for*
> *my celebration of _____).*

Your Book of Shadows Notes

Spells

Sometimes, the effect of a spell will be astonishingly immediate. Sometimes, you will have to wait for a while. Be patient and believe in your spell. Repeat your spell if you see no effect after two weeks, making the second spell stronger. If you still see no effect, you can assume the spell was not in accord with the universe and move on to something else. If it is something that's too important for you to drop, try approaching the problem from another direction.

◇◇◇

Eileen Holland, *The Wicca Handbook*

Wheel of the Year with Places to Fill In Your Goals for Each Season

The Wheel of the Year is basically the Pagan calendar in the round. It includes all eight sabbats, each of which has its own special energy. One great thing you can do in your Book of Shadows is to use the wheel to track your goals for the year. This fun diagram can help you do that, and you can color it as you go!

I find it helpful to start the year with an overall goal and then break it down into more manageable pieces. The eight seasons can really help with this. For instance, say my goal for the year is to be more productive with my writing. (Seriously, this is my plan for every year.) I might make overall plans at Imbolc, plant the seeds for more productivity at the Spring Equinox by listing ways I can be more efficient, figure out people who can be useful partners in my endeavors at Beltane, and so on. During the harvest seasons I might check in on my progress and regroup if I'm not achieving what I'd hoped to. Sometimes my original goals don't work and I have to shift and change. That's okay. You just might want to use pencil while filling in your own goals!

Spells

List of Plans for Each Goal
and a Place to Track Progress

It is important to have goals, both magical and practical everyday life ones. Magical goals may include getting more practice at various aspects of our Craft, becoming more familiar with tools or deities or forms of divination, or simply integrating our witchcraft more deeply into our daily lives. Practical goals are more likely to be things like finding love, increasing prosperity, or working on healing.

All of these things can be achieved with spellwork, but it can be easy to lose track of our intentions in the midst of our busy lives. Writing down goals can serve as a reminder of what we want to work on, as well as giving us a way to keep track of what we have already done and what we still wish to accomplish.

Some people like to make focus boards with pictures that represent their goals for the year and hang the boards where they can see them often. But a Book of Shadows is a perfect place to write down and track your magical goals and the progress you've made toward achieving them.

You can start with a new year, a new season, or simply whenever the goal becomes important. This chart is one possible way to put your intent and focus into physical form—and then follow up with actual magical work, of course.

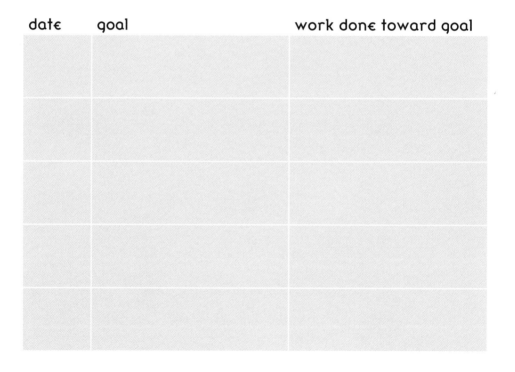

date	goal	work done toward goal

date	goal	work done toward goal

Spell Creation Checklist and Fillable Grid

Alternately, you can keep track of the spells you do using this chart.

DATE/ OCCASION	SPELL TITLE AND AUTHOR	SPELL GOAL
example: full moon		

Tools	Deities Invoked	Other	Results
selenite wand		full moon bath	

Fill In Your Own Spells

Here is a place to write down the spells you've written or those by others you used.

Every spell is a journey.

❖

Lawren Leo, *Love's Shadow:*
Nine Crooked Paths

Five Simple Spells for Daily Use

It is always a good idea to have a few basic spells in your pocket that you can use for various things. (Well, maybe not in your actual pocket, but at least in your Book of Shadows.)

What kinds of spells you need will depend on your own life. For instance, I tend to get bad headaches, and on my worst days I'll take some ibuprofen in an effort to take the worst of it away. When I do, I use this spell:

God and Goddess, hear my plea

Take this pain away from me

Leaving me feeling good instead

Strong of body, clear of head

As you can see, it is short and simple so I can recite it from memory, and if I happen to be around non-witchy people, I can say it in my head.

Your daily spells, whatever they are, should probably also be something short and easy to remember, and something that you would use often. It's up to you whether or not you would want to do any sort of ritual with these, like lighting a candle. But usually these kinds of spells are something you just say as needed.

If you are someone who has to travel often, you might want a "safe travels" spell. If you worry when you send your kids out to school, you might want a protection blessing to say every day when they walk out the door. It is very individual.

If you feel comfortable writing your own spells, this is an excellent place to start. If not, you can look through spell books written by other people to see if you can find the ones that would suit you best. Then write them down here so you will have them handy.

Spell for _____

Spell for _____

....

....

....

....

....

....

....

....

....

....

....

....

....

....

....

....

....

....

....

....

....

....

....

....

....

....

Spell for _____

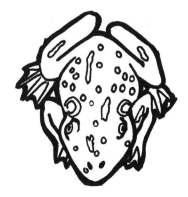

Spell for _____

Spell for _____

Full Moon Spells

You will also want to have a few handy full moon spells, especially if you are like me and tend to look at the calendar and say, "Wait, it's the full moon *tonight*?!" While we often do specific magical work on the full moon, sometimes it is nice to just walk outside or stand at your altar and commune with the Goddess. Like the daily spells, these can be kept short and simple so they can be memorized, although there is nothing wrong with reading a spell out of a book or off of a piece of paper. (I've gotten terrible at memorizing things as I've gotten older, so anything longer than about four to six lines usually gets written down. I promise, the gods don't care.)

Full moon spells are generally directed at the Goddess, since it is her night, although you can also just say them to the universe in general.

Unlike spells with a magical goal, these types of full moon spells are mostly just a way of greeting the Goddess or reinforcing your identity as a witch or generally acknowledging the magic inherent in the changing cycles of the moon. There is no wrong way to do them, and you can always make something up on the spot if you prefer.

Here's one simple example that I use. Sometimes I go outside to look at the moon, and sometimes (especially if there is a foot of snow on the ground) I light a candle at my altar and stand there for a while, just feeling her presence.

Great Goddess, I greet you on this, the night of
your full moon, and ask for your blessing.

Shine your light on me and illuminate my path.
Hold me in your loving arms
and watch over me in the days to come.

Great Goddess, I greet you and thank you
for your presence in my life.

Blessed be!

As with the daily spells, you can either write your own or copy down a few you particularly like here.

Full Moon Spell 1

....
....
....
....
....
....
....
....

Full Moon Spell 2

....
....
....
....
....
....
....
....

Full Moon Spell 3

....
....
....
....
....
....
....
....

Magick is within and around us at
all times; all it takes is the ability to
acknowledge and connect with it.

❖

Mat Auryn, *Mastering Magick:*
A Course in Spellcasting for the Psychic Witch

Spells

144

A Witch's Guide to Chakras

You have probably heard of chakras, but you might not know exactly what they are or how they are used in the practice of witchcraft. The chakras are energy centers of the body that affect physical, mental, and emotional health and well-being. The beliefs surrounding them originated with Buddhist and Hindu practices but are now also common among those who fall under the wide New Age umbrella.

I have worked with them for years in my practice as a healer and have had other healers work on mine, and I can tell you that I believe in them completely, just in case you weren't sure.

You can think of the chakras as centers of power in the body. There are seven major chakras, each of them associated with a color as well as specific issues or parts of the body they affect. As usual, not every book you read will agree on exactly what these all are, but here's a basic chart to help guide you.

CHAKRA	COLOR	LOCATION	REPRESENTS	INFLUENCE
Crown	Purple, white	Top of the head	Joy, spirituality, connection to the universe and deity	Brain, nervous system
Third Eye	Indigo	Center of forehead between eyes	Insight, intuition, wisdom, psychic abilities	Eyes, nose
Throat	Blue	Base of throat	Communication, truth, creativity	Throat, mouth, thyroid
Heart	Green	Center of chest	Love, empathy, compassion	Heart, circulatory system
Solar Plexus	Yellow	Right above navel	Strength, power, self-confidence, courage	Digestive system, adrenal gland
Sacral	Orange	Lower abdomen under navel	Passion, joy, sexuality, creativity, playfulness	Reproductive system, kidneys, bladder
Root	Red	Base of the spine	Grounding, survival, centering	Spine, legs, male reproductive system

If the chakras are fully open and all the energy flows from one to another freely, life is good. Unfortunately, many things can cause the chakras to close up or the energy not to flow well, so it is a good idea to occasionally check in with those power centers and make sure they are okay. Energy healers sometimes use crystals to help open and boost the chakras, which is something you can do for yourself if you have the right stones. You can also put your hands over each chakra spot one at a time and open up your intuition to anything that doesn't seem right. This can take some practice, so don't feel intimidated if you can't sense anything when you first start. You can write down anything you feel or do here.

You might want to look up which stones are associated with each chakra, for instance, and make a note of them.

CHAKRA	STONES
Crown	
Third Eye	
Throat	
Heart	
Solar Plexus	
Sacral	
Root	

....

....

....

....

....

....

....

....

Chakra Spell for
Balancing and Strengthening

This spell will work best if you can visualize each chakra as you say the spell. Not everyone is good at visualizing, though, and if you're one of those folks who isn't, you can just look at a picture that shows them all laid out. It may also be helpful to put your hand or hands on each chakra as you go through the spell.

If you want to really go all out, you can get seven candles, one in each of the chakra colors, and light them as you say the spell. (Note that some people use white for the crown chakra instead of purple, and use light purple for the third eye. Whatever you feel is right will work.) Otherwise, you can just light a single white candle. They even sell candles that have all the colors in one.

This is a good spell to do if you are just feeling "off" or sluggish.

Head to toe and toe to head

Open and release, cleanse and connect

Crown, open to spirit and clarity

Third eye, open to intuition and clear vision

Throat, open to communication and guidance

Heart, open to love and hope

Solar plexus, open to emotion and will

Sacral, open to creativity and energy

Root, open to grounding and stability

Open and release all that holds me back

*Let energy flow freely from top to
bottom and back again*

*Let me be balanced and healthy in
all my centers of power*

So mote it be

Take a minute to visualize all the chakra centers swirling in the same direction in unison. Sit with this image as long as feels right to you.

Keeping the energy centers we call chakras open
and balanced is absolutely essential to being
intuitive and also being healthy and fully alive.

❖

Catherine Carrigan, *What Is Healing?*
Awaken Your Intuitive Power for Health and Happiness

Your Book of Shadows Notes

Magical Recipes

Applying mindfulness to food can reconnect you
with the ingredients, thereby deepening
your connection to the earth.

❖❖❖

Dawn Aurora Hunt,
Kitchen Witchcraft for Beginners

Common Ingredients and Their Uses

We've already talked about which herbs are most useful in the kitchen, both for kitchen magic and just plain cooking, but there is more to kitchen witchery than herbs. Many of the foods we use every day have magical associations, which you can use for planning meals that center around a certain magical goal or just to add that extra intentional touch to a special meal.

For instance, most grains, such as wheat, oats, and rice, are associated with prosperity, as are beans and nuts. Dairy products like milk and butter are often associated with love and spirituality. Here is a short list of common kitchen ingredients and their associations, with spaces underneath for you to add your own additional favorites if they aren't included here.

- ✧ Almonds: healing, prosperity
- ✧ Apple: love, health, peace
- ✧ Banana: prosperity, love
- ✧ Beans: prosperity, sex
- ✧ Beer: protection
- ✧ Black pepper: protection, purification
- ✧ Blueberries: protection
- ✧ Broccoli: protection
- ✧ Butter: spirituality

153

- ✧ Cayenne pepper: creativity, protection
- ✧ Chocolate: love, prosperity
- ✧ Coffee: energy, intellect
- ✧ Eggs: healing, protection, divination, fertility
- ✧ Honey: purification, healing, love, happiness, spirituality, wisdom
- ✧ Lemon/lime/orange: love, purification
- ✧ Lettuce: prosperity, peace
- ✧ Milk: love, spirituality
- ✧ Olives/olive oil: health, peace
- ✧ Onion: protection
- ✧ Peanuts: prosperity
- ✧ Peppers: protection
- ✧ Potatoes: protection
- ✧ Rice: prosperity, fertility, protection
- ✧ Salt: grounding, protection
- ✧ Spinach: prosperity
- ✧ Strawberry: love
- ✧ Sugar: love
- ✧ Tea: prosperity, courage, intellect
- ✧ Tomatoes: healing, prosperity, love, protection
- ✧ Vinegar: purification, protection
- ✧ Wheat: prosperity
- ✧ Wine: celebration
- ✧ _____
- ✧ _____
- ✧ _____
- ✧ _____
- ✧ _____
- ✧ _____
- ✧ _____

Some Witches are confirmed meat eaters, while others follow a vegetarian or vegan path; sometimes this is for spiritual or ethical reasons, health, or concern for our planet since it is an established fact that raising meat takes more energy and causes more damage than raising plants. This is a personal choice that each person has to make for themselves. If you're not sure, ask the gods for guidance or try each path to see which one feels right to you.

Quick and Easy Recipes
with Magical Uses

You can turn any meal into magic by adding intent and the right ingredients. Here are a couple quick examples. Using the ingredients above, the herbs we talked about earlier, and any other foods you care to research (or follow your gut feeling about), you can create your own magical recipes.

Here are two simple examples to get you started.

Healing Omelet: Eggs themselves are healing, as are many herbs that you can add to them, such as rosemary. If you cook your omelet in olive oil, that just adds another healing element.

Prosperity Pesto: Pesto is made primarily from basil leaves and pine nuts, both of which are potent prosperity foods. I like to add a little parsley to mine for an extra boost.

Keep in mind that you can also make a recipe that has more than one purpose, combining elements for protection with those for prosperity, and so on. Intent is at least as important as the ingredients you choose, and cooking with love—even if it is just for yourself—is a kind of magic in and of itself.

Fill In Your Own Recipes

Your Book of Shadows Notes

....
....
....
....
....
....
....
....
....
....
....
....
....
....
....
....
....
....
....
....
....
....
....
....

Healing/
Peace

Protection

Love

Prosperity/
Abundance

Correspondences

There is a dance. The dance moves throughout the universe, throughout the galaxy, throughout the planets, throughout the Earth, throughout the Earth's creations . . . crystals, plants, trees, people, you. In this dance within you and within everything in the universe, there is a single energy, the music, creating a connectivity between the participants.

❖

Sally Dubats, *Natural Magick:*
The Essential Witch's Grimoire

All things are connected, and all energy is connected. This is part of why correspondences are used in magic—so that one small piece of the whole can stand for and represent a much larger energy. Thus a piece of tiger's eye can connect you to the energy of courage, and sage can be used to purify and heal. Working with correspondences is part of a witch's tool kit, and the more of them you know, the more different kinds of magical work you can give that special boost.

Many witches keep track of correspondences in their Book of Shadows, both in a general way and as a part of their own spells and rituals. I gave a few examples in *The Eclectic Witch's Book of Shadows,* and I'll start you off with one more here. Then you can begin to add your own as you follow your personal journey.

Correspondences can be found online and in books (I get a lot of mine from authors like Scott Cunningham, Dorothy Morrison, and the like). You will find that different sources rarely agree on which specific items do what, so to some extent you are going to have to listen to your own instincts and inner wisdom, which isn't a bad thing at all.

You also don't have to use all the different kinds of correspondences I list. If, for instance, you don't use rune symbols, don't bother to write those down. As always, just do whatever works for you.

Strength and Courage

Gods and Goddesses: Ares, Artemis, Diana, Inanna, Isis, Shanti, Tyr

Stones: agate (especially orange and red), amethyst, carnelian, citrine, lapis, tiger's eye

Herbs: allspice, apple, basil, cinnamon, clove, frankincense, lemon, patchouli, pine, sage, thyme

Colors: bright yellow, orange, red

Rune symbols: Uruz, Kenaz, Sigel

....

....

....

....

....

....

....

....

....

....

....

....

....

....

....

....

Cleansing and Purification

Gods and Goddesses:

Stones:

Herbs:

Colors:

Rune symbols:

....
....
....
....
....
....
....
....
....
....
....
....
....
....
....
....
....

Increase Power

Gods and Goddesses:

Stones:

Herbs:

Colors:

Rune Symbols:

....
....
....
....
....
....
....
....
....
....
....
....
....
....
....
....

Psychic Abilities

Gods and Goddesses:

Stones:

Herbs:

Colors:

Rune symbols:

....

....

....

....

....

....

....

....

....

....

....

....

....

....

....

....

....

Your Book of Shadows Notes

One Final Note

I hope you have found this workbook to be helpful, both as a companion to the original *Eclectic Witch's Book of Shadows* and on its own. May you continue to use it in the years to come in good health, with joy, and with ever-growing knowledge. May you walk your magical path in light and love.

Deborah

About the Artist

© TRISTAN FOX MUELLER

Mickie Mueller has been a practicing witch for over twenty years. She's illustrated multiple tarot and oracle decks, and her illustrations have appeared in various Llewellyn books and periodicals since 2007, many also featuring articles written by Mickie. Art is a magickal process for her, and she uses various methods to infuse her work with magickal intentions. In addition to her art, she is also an author and presents practical witchcraft tutorials on YouTube. She makes her home in Missouri, where she and her husband, Dan, sell her art all over the world. Find more of Mickie's art at

MICKIEMUELLERSTUDIO.ETSY.COM